Witches

Brandon Robshaw
and
Rochelle Scholar

Published in association with The Basic Skills Agency

Hodder & Stoughton

A MEMBER OF THE HODDER HEADLINE GROUP

Acknowledgements
Cover artwork: Jaroslav
Illustrations: Bridget Dowty
Photos: p. 7 © Bettman/Corbis; p. 11 © AKG Photo London; p.14 © Topham Picturepoint.

With thanks to Rosaria Trenta.

Every effort has been made to trace copyright holders of material reproduced in this book.
Any rights not acknowledged will be acknowledged in subsequent printings if notice is given
to the publisher.

Orders: please contact Bookpoint Ltd, 130 Milton Park, Abingdon, Oxon OX14 4SB.
Telephone: (44) 01235 827720, Fax: (44) 01235 400454. Lines are open from 9.00 – 6.00,
Monday to Saturday, with a 24 hour message answering service. Email address:
orders@bookpoint.co.uk

British Library Cataloguing in Publication Data
A catalogue record for this title is available from The British Library

ISBN 0 340 84863 4

First published 2002
Impression number   10 9 8 7 6 5 4 3 2 1
Year   2007 2006 2005 2004 2003 2002

Copyright © 2002 Brandon Robshaw and Rochelle Scholar

Typeset by SX Composing DTP, Rayleigh, Essex.
Printed in Great Britain for Hodder & Stoughton Educational, a division of Hodder
Headline Plc, 338 Euston Road, London NW1 3BH by The Bath Press Ltd.

Contents

Rosie – a modern witch.

1   Rosie

Rosie is a witch.
She doesn't fly around on a broomstick.
She doesn't wear a black pointed hat.
She doesn't have a black cat.

You wouldn't know she was a witch
unless you looked at her closely.
Around her neck Rosie wears a five-pointed star.
Around the star is a circle.
The necklace is a sign of her faith.

Rosie is a modern witch.

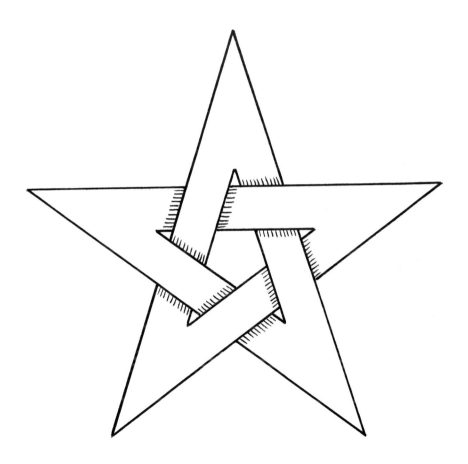

The five-pointed star, a sign of faith for witches.

2 Good Witches and Bad Witches

Rosie lives in London.
She works in an office.
Rosie says she uses her powers
and her spells every day.
She says she would sometimes like
to put a spell on her boss!

As Rosie says, 'If I didn't believe in it
I wouldn't do it. It's not hocus-pocus.
I know my spells work.'

But being a witch is not
just about doing spells and magic.
It is a way of life.

Both men and women can be witches.
Nurses, doctors, teachers, police officers.
People from all walks of life do witchcraft.

There are good witches and bad witches,
just as there are good people and bad people.

Rosie is open about being a witch.
But she knows people who have lost their jobs
because others do not understand
what being a witch means.

People from all wolks of life can be witches.

3 A Bad Press

For a long time,
witches have had a bad press.
In old stories, witches are always evil.
Like the witch in the story of
Hansel and Gretel.
She caught and planned to eat
the two children.
Or the three witches in
Shakespeare's play *Macbeth*.
They cooked up evil spells together,
putting things like toads' eyes and
frogs' toes into their pot.

Nearer our own time there was
the Wicked Witch of the West
in *The Wizard of Oz*.

The Wicked Witch of the West with Dorothy in *The Wizard of Oz*.

All this has nothing to do
with what real witches are like.
But the fear of witches
goes back a long way.

In 1486, by order of the Church,
witches were hunted and killed.
People thought that witches
prayed to the Devil.

This idea came from the Church.
The Church said that if a person
did not believe in Christ,
then they believed in the Devil.

Rosie says that a lot of midwives at this time
were accused of being witches.
She says, 'The midwife would help
the woman in labour with herbs.
The men couldn't understand this.
They thought it was witchcraft.'

In Europe from 1486 to the 1700s
thousands of people were hunted out.
They were burnt to death,
stoned, drowned and hanged
because people thought they were witches.
Many of these people were not witches.

In 1604, James I of England
passed the Witchcraft Act.
Anyone found using witchcraft was hanged.
In 1692, this act was used
in witch trials in Salem, America.

4 The Salem Witch Trials

Salem is a small town
in New England, America.
In 1692, it was a deeply Christian community.
A number of girls and young women,
aged between nine and 20 years old,
said that people in Salem
were putting spells on them.
They accused four people.
A female slave.
A poor woman.
A disabled widow.
The mother of a mixed-race child.

These four women were put on trial.
At the trials the accusers would
cry out in pain and have fits.

Many people were drowned because they were
thought to be witches.

Soon, they began to accuse more people
of being witches.

Then two of the accusers said that
they had made it all up.
They were then accused
of being witches themselves.
By the end of The Witch Trials,
19 people, 13 of them women,
had been hanged.
One old man
was crushed to death with rocks.
Two more people died in prison.

Fourteen years after The Witch Trials,
the youngest accuser
said the people she had accused
were innocent.

5   Different Types of Witches

Today, there are many
different types of witches.
Some witches work in groups.
A group of witches is called a coven.

There are between three and 20
witches in a coven.
Most covens have a High Priestess
and a High Priest.

Rosie does not work in a coven.
She prefers to work alone.

Gerald Gardner, founder of the Gardenerian tradition.

Witches can also choose to follow
different witchcraft traditions.

One tradition is called the Gardnerians.
This is named after a man
called Gerald Gardner.
In England, in the 1950s,
Gerald Gardner went public
about his witchcraft.

Gardnerians work without clothes on.
They call this 'going skyclad'.

6 Wicca

Rosie is a Wiccan witch.
Wiccan witches have a deep belief
in the power of nature.

Wicca is a religion that uses
magic and rituals.
Wiccan witches do not try
to convert people to their religion.

Wiccan witches do not work
with evil powers.
Wiccans believe that they must
act for the good of all.

Wiccans worship the 'All'.
The All is both male and female.
Wiccans believe the female spirit
made the male spirit.
Witches choose to call upon
many gods and goddesses
who are part of the All.

One of the most important rules of Wicca is:
'If it harms none, do what you will.'

This means that a witch should
cause no harm to anyone.
We are here to live in peace
with each other and with nature.

7   Wiccan Rituals

Like most religions, Wicca has rituals.
There are moon rituals
to celebrate the Goddess.
Witches get together to chant and say prayers
to the Goddess.

Rosie says, 'It is important to celebrate the Goddess
at least once a month.' .

Before a ritual, witches fast.
They take a ritual bath
and then put on a special gown.
Some witches go 'skyclad'.
Rosie doesn't.
She says she is too shy!

An altar set up for a Wiccan ritual.

Before the ritual begins, the altar is set up.
Ritual tools, such as a knife and a cup,
are put on the altar.

The ritual is held in a magic circle.
If you have to leave the magic circle
you must cut a door in the energy.
The witch's broom is left by the door
to guard the room.

These moon rituals are called 'Esbats'.
They celebrate the female energy of the All.

There are also rituals to celebrate
the male energy of the All.
They happen eight times a year,
at festivals called Sabbats.

8 Magic

Wiccan witches use their
magic power for the good of all.
Magic means using energy
to change something.

Witches believe that a full moon
has a lot of power.
The full moon of each month
has its own name.

But a witch can work with
any phase of the moon.
When a witch 'draws down the moon'
she believes that she gets power
from the Goddess.

Witches use many magic tools.
Rosie uses a wand that she bought in a shop.
She says, 'You can use anything as your wand,
even a stick.'

Crystal balls are used to pull in energy.
A broom is used to sweep away bad energy.

Some witches do use black magic.
This is when a witch uses their energy
to harm someone.

Rosie is against black magic.
She says, 'If you do a bad spell
– a spell causing harm to someone –
it will come back on you three times as bad.'

9 Spells

A spell is like a magic recipe.
'If you want to use spells,' says Rosie,
'you also have to make an effort . . .
Nothing comes for free.
If you want something
you have to work at it too.'

Witches learn how to write their own spells.
There are spells that can
draw good things to you,
such as love and luck.

A witch should never charge money for a spell.

Before a Wiccan witch uses magic spells,
they have to be sure that
no one is going to get hurt.
Spells should not affect a person's free will.

For example, if you use a love spell
you cannot make someone
fall in love with you.
But you could use a love spell
to make yourself more attractive.

Many people like to have protection spells.
A protection spell keeps bad energy away.
There are also binding spells.
A binding spell can be used
to stop a person's bad behaviour.

10 The Book of Shadows

Witches write all their spells
in their 'Book of Shadows'.
This book is a kind of magic diary.

Each coven also has its own Book of Shadows.
Nowadays a witch may keep
her Book of Shadows on a computer.

When a witch dies, their Book of Shadows
is burnt or buried with them.
Sometimes a witch
leaves their book to another witch.

A Book of Shadows.

11 Summerland

Wiccan witches do not
believe in heaven or hell.
They believe that when they die
they go to a place called Summerland.

Summerland is where
spirits go after death to rest.
They think about the lives they have just lived.

Some spirits sleep, but others are restless.
These restless spirits want to
get back to earth.

Wiccans believe in rebirth.
Rosie says, 'We all have
things to learn and
things to teach on this earth.'

So now you know.
Witches do not ride on broomsticks.
They do not have black cats.
They do not wear black hats.
Witches are ordinary people.
They may be nurses, doctors,
policemen or teachers.
Your teacher, or next-door neighbour,
could be a witch!

If they are, there is no need to worry.
The most important rule of Wicca
is one we could all live by:
'If it harms none, do what you will.'